KHALILAH SLEEPOVER

LATOSHA NELLON

Print information available on the last page

Rev. date: 04/24/2019

To order additional copies of this book, contact:
Xlibris
1-888-795-4274
www.Xlibris.com
Orders@Xlibris.com

KHALILAH SLEEPOVER

Today is the day it's my 9th birthday. I'm very excited to have my sleep over. All my friends from school will be here. My mom has a lot of activity planned for us. She has our game room setup like a spa .We can get our nails and our feet done. My dad is on the grill I can see the smoke from the window. He's cooking hamburgers and hotdogs two of my favorite foods. This sleepover will be the best ever. I plan to stay up dancing all night.

My mom has made sure everyone has a sleeping bag. She also made candy bags for the girls to take home. Our house is decorated in purple everything, even down to my cake it's a chocolate cake with chocolate icing and purple crystals on it. Of course with all that chocolate we will have vanilla ice cream. Along with hot chips and cotton candy. Oh my look at the time. I should be getting dressed right now. The girls should be arriving any minute. I have the cutest pj's its purple with my name on it . My mom had it made . I think I heard the doorbell.

Yes it was the doorbell, its my bestfriend she just walking in the door as I was walking downstairs. I'm very excited to see her and show her the house. Here Khalilah this is your birthday gift. Thanks Aniyah let's put your things in the living room and we can head over to the spa.

The spa yes my mom has the gameroom set up for us. Wow how cool is that .We can start getting our nails done while we are waiting for the other girls. As we were getting our nails done the girls started to show up . They were all surprised when they saw the spa. The look on their faces was priceless. I know my party will be the talk of school come Monday morning.

After all the girls got their nails done
we decided to go to the living room
and eat and watch a few movies.

After the movies we dance our little hearts out.

We didn't fall asleep until 2am .We jumped, flipped, hopped whatever you could think of we did it. I will never forget this sleepover it was the best ever.

As all of us started waking up my mom had breakfast waiting for us. There was champagne glasses with girts in it and a smaller plate with bacon, eggs and fruit on it with our choice of drinks. We all enjoyed our breakfast while waiting for parents to show up. One by one the girls started to leave. I handed them their candy bags as I walked them to the door. Giving them hugs and saying thank you once more.

As I closed the door on the last girl leaving.
My mom asked me how was I feeling. Words
couldn't explain this wonderful feeling.
Turning 9 was just the beginning.

Printed in the United States
By Bookmasters